Content and Copywrit

I0062163

Learn SEO Content Writing and How to Create a Compelling Promotional Content to Win More Clients

By

GoldInk Books

BEFORE YOU START READING, DOWNLOAD YOUR FREE DIGITAL ASSETS!

Be sure to visit the URL below on your computer or mobile device to access the free digital asset files that are included with your purchase of this book.

These digital assets will complement the material in the book and are referenced throughout the text.

DOWNLOAD YOURS HERE:

www.GoldInkBooks.com

The trademarks that are used are without any consent, and the publication of the trademark is without permission or backing by the trademark owner. All trademarks and brands within this book are for clarifying purposes only and are owned by the owners themselves, not affiliated with this document.

Table of Contents

Introduction

SEO (Search Engine Optimization) experts and copywriters have a dirty little secret that they do not want you to know. No matter what they say, their vested interests lie in keeping their wealth of knowledge out of reach. While a number of professional copywriters do offer coaching or training, it comes at a hefty price. But you cannot honestly blame them, can you? Even the most unknown but decent copywriters earn so much per assignment that you would think they have themselves a money-making machine, and it only gets better as they move up the ranks. However, we understand that writing for oneself is much different than writing for other people. The latter means that you have to extensively study and examine their product as well as their market. It also means that you have to be familiar with the ins and outs of Search Engine Optimization, which is both intimidating and confusing. There is so much to learn and so little idea where to start from. Interestingly, if you are somebody with an established online business and a website ,that's up and running, you may still feel that your sales have suddenly dropped or your website does not show up in the search results the way it used to do.

We are here to tell you; we have been there and understand your struggle; therefore, I will provide you with solutions instead of just offering a listening ear. From Copywriting and SEO basics to numerous Copywriting secrets, tricks, and tips collected from my vast experience, you are in excellent hands. To tell you more about myself, my deep knowledge about copywriting and extensive experience means that the span of my research on marketing copywriting is ceaseless.

Therefore, it is no wonder I am one of the first few people who have contributed to the concept of "Copywriting and its importance for a business." I believe that whether you are a beginner or an expert, it is never too late to learn, and there is always room to learn more. Therefore, this book not only touches the basics of SEO and copywriting but also dives into relatively advanced knowledge on SEO. Simply put, everyone has something to take away from this gold mine of knowledge because no matter what stage they are at, they have to connect with their clients and draw traffic towards their online business. To tell you how I will go about these vast subjects and start at the grassroots, explaining to you what SEO is, what copywriting is, and how they are related. This is followed by guidelines on how to optimize your content.

Once that is understood, you dive into the world of copywriting myths and are shocked to find out how many of them you actually believed. However, it is not your fault; all copywriters, including me, have been in your shoes at some point. Knowing this, I demystify each misconception ranging from 'copywriting is just writing' to 'copywriting is selling.' Next, we explore the ultimate copywriting formula HOBO. This secret formula is the crux of great copywriting. It is followed by a list of super helpful theories and secret formulas, including the four universal strokes to incur good sales fortune, the benefit explosion system, and the art of headline swiping. You are also made familiar with excelling sale approaches and learn the inner workings of Search engine optimization. This chapter is especially important for amateurs or those who wish to revise their knowledge of search engine optimization and learn more. Further, we will divulge the secrets to writing high-impact sales copy. This part will focus on stimulating the reader's imagination and then pushing it into a direction from where they can purchase your product. This is primarily done through the headlines, which make the reader either imagine themselves in a state of complete bliss or evoke the need to be successful. This is followed by the 7 fool-proof principles to do great copywriting.

I ensure that these are not just run-of-the-mill points, but a fresher perspective among the sea of SEO guides available online. Then gradually coming full circle, I will go into the specifications of writing a winning sales letter and tell you how the different parts of the letter, from the introduction to the statement of benefit, fit together like a puzzle and are incomplete without the other. You are also introduced to instant sales letter templates for days when you have too much to write in very little time. Lastly, we will bring home the fact that all writers face creativity blocks regardless of how talented they are, and it is nothing to be anxious about; all they need is a few simple mental exercises to get their creativity flowing. This is followed by expert tips on improving your SEO and copywriting skills.

However, through all of the above, you will never feel that I am merely imparting bookish knowledge that has no substance in real life. Instead, the language used is simple; whatever tips and tricks I have given are backed by the trial and test of several other experts in the field. Moreover, the book is a gold mine of copywriting secrets that you are unlikely to find elsewhere, but none of which are hollow claims. It is backed by examples that even people who know nothing about SEO will understand.

It is easy to get off track when talking about the vast SEO world because there is just so much you can teach. Therefore, to keep it simple for you, the book has been streamlined to touch all relevant topics without making it overly complex. Moving towards the end of this book, you will realize that you never really stopped reading because at no point did it get too overwhelming or outlandish. Therefore, if you are ready to place your trust in my expertise and are ready to boost your business through the knowledge of SEO copywriting, it is time to start reading.

Chapter 1: Do You Really Need SEO and Copywriting to Develop a Company?

This chapter will give you an insight into the essentials of SEO Copywriting and explain its role in the marketing process.

1.1 The Basics of SEO Copywriting

Before discussing the value of SEO copywriting, let's discuss its definition; what is SEO?

Search Engine Optimization (SEO) is a discipline that works to enhance the quality and quantity of traffic coming to your website. In total, there are 3 types of SEO that one can become familiar with.

- On-page SEO consists of optimizing a website's content to increase its chances of it being discovered by search engines and users. This is also the core of SEO copywriting.

- Off-page SEO involves activities that are performed away from one's website yet affect their rankings. For example, social shares, link building, and others.

- Technical SEO deals with the technical aspects of your website. These include indexation, crawl budget, crawlability , and more.

While the first and second types of search engine optimization help your website gain a high rank compared to other websites, the problem arises when these websites are equal in terms of technical SEO. At this point, you will require solid SEO copywriting skills and strategy to gain the upper hand.

What is SEO Copywriting?

SEO copywriting is the science and art of making online content which both people and search engines love. This content will rank well on SERPs or search engine result pages.

People who visit your website would also find its content engaging and informative, making it easier for your website to achieve its goals. While SEO copywriting writing needs to have the content that Google understands, it also should be the content that the audience would want to link, read, and share.

Therefore, if you write content that is only for Google, it will begin to sound immensely robotic. However, if your content is only for your readers, your webpage would not contain essential keywords used by people. Therefore, it is a tricky balance to strike, but one that you need to master if you want to excel at SEO in 2021.

What makes good SEO copywriting?

It is sometimes hard to differentiate between SEO copywriting and just good copywriting because both need to be error-free, appealing to the audience, and benefits-led. But SEO content would be optimized using certain keywords which should look natural and not stuffed artificial.

Present-day SEO techniques work by giving each web page suitable title tags and ensuring that their content is not low-quality. Meaning it should be original, grammatically correct, factual, authoritative, and engaging for users. Another important part of SEO copywriting today is quality link building with credible sites. This means that if your website is linked with external sites, there is more chance that your content will rank higher for certain keywords. (SEO copywriting: The definitive guide, 2020)

To sum it up, these are the 5 most essential elements in SEO copywriting:

1) Headlines

The headline on your webpage is one of the most crucial elements of the SEO copy because it grabs people's attention and motivates them to keep on clicking and reading further.

Below are four tips that can be used to write snappy headlines:

- Include a number in the headline if possible. It has been found that titles with numbers tend to have higher click-through rates.

- Keep the headline short. Search engines display titles only up to 72 characters. Therefore, avoid long and meandering headlines as much as possible.

- For content inspiration, use Google. Look for the target keywords and keep an eye out for themes appearing in the content, topics, and headlines which show up in the search. This will tell you what the hottest topics are, i.e., those receiving the greatest traffic.

- Use Yoast SEO. This WordPress plugin aids you in optimizing your content by using a ranking system that is easy to understand.

2) Meta descriptions

These are text-based short descriptions of what is on your page. Here are some tips for writing compelling descriptions.

a) Keep it under 150 characters (including spaces)

b) For pages on mobile, keep your meta descriptions below 113 characters (including spaces).

c) Make sure that your description describes what your page is all about and also includes a call-to-action so that readers are encouraged to click and learn more.

d) Add your target keywords in the description. If these match with the audience's search query, they will be shown in bold, indicating that a page is relevant to their needs and interests.

e) Try to write different descriptions across the entire site. Otherwise, Google and other search engines tend to 'flag' your descriptions as duplicate content and do not rank your webpage as high.

3) Content

When someone is looking up something on a search engine, they are searching for content that meets their needs, and it is through SEO copywriting, we create this high-quality content that gives them their desired results.

The key to writing high-ranking SEO content

Before you begin to write, it is crucial to understand **who you are writing for.**

Keep your customers in mind and question yourself: what sort of queries could I answer for these people? The truth is that the more specialized "niche" you have, the greater the likelihood of your content showing up on SERP.

4) Keyword frequency and density

Keyword frequency means how often the target keywords appear on the reader's page, while keyword density talks about the ratio of a keyword phrase to other words on that page.

If you are writing a post of 1000 words and your target phrase is "professional Manitoba photographer", — density refers to the number of times that phrase appears and how frequently it is used compared to other words on your page.

If you overdo it, this is known as "keyword stuffing," and jamming a phrase of keyword into the text too many times, which causes your page to be flagged as "spam, by search engines and makes your content look suspicious as well.

Here is an example:

"Looking for the greatest professional San Jose photographer? You are at the right place. We provide the best-quality professional San Jose photography at competitive rates. Want to know about our professional San Jose photography services? Click here."

Not great, right?

The example shows how suspicious jamming looks, but if you are unsure about your keyword-to-content ratio, you can use the SEO book keyword density tool.

5) Page links

Page Links help search engines view that your webpage is connected to the rest of the web and if your content is relevant enough to lead to other relevant content.

While no "hard and fast" rules exist regarding page linking, here are some you can keep in mind:

- Link to suitable pages within your own site

- Link to detailed 3rd party resources and guides.

- Link to other web pages that have appropriate anchor text which sounds natural (Shane, 2021)

1.2 Why Does Your Business Need SEO Copy Writing?

Being the first means being the best

Your goal is to receive the highest ranking in search engines which will give your website more visibility. Therefore, you need to be listed among the topmost results in search engine pages (SERPS). When people look for certain products and services by typing keywords in Google or other engines, they mostly go to the topmost result. This is because results on the first page are considered to be best associated with the targeted keywords. While people see several other pages and the total number of results is also shown, they tend to stick to the first page if they are looking for a specific answer.

To compete with businesses online, you should always aim for the number one spot as your final goal, not the third or fourth spot.

Moreover, having the first rank means that you have at least a 32.5% share of the traffic, while being second means you are at 17.6% and third, means you only have 11.4% of the traffic coming to your page.

Traffic essentially means that more people are reading, viewing, sharing, and being inspired by the content on your page.

Your business gains respectability

While it is good to focus on a larger picture, we must not neglect the importance of the viewers.

As the owner of a business, you want your viewers to trust your brand. According to a number of researches, at least 82% of B2B customers wish to get more information about a business before purchasing from it.

This information can have a positive impact and convince the buyers to purchase a product, and it can also have the opposite effect. This means that it is critical to keep a good reputation as a business no matter what you are selling.

Therefore, SEO copywriting makes your business appear more professional and trustworthy; it makes your page more accessible and engages and informs the readers. The outcome is valuable content and a solid audience.

Words sell

One should never underestimate the magnitude of words. It is true that within online marketing, the whole image of business matters; not only should your website be aesthetically pleasing, but it should also have a logical structure and a convenient navigation system. However, you can also sell a business using the power of your words. Therefore, ensure that your content serves the right purpose by attracting potential customers and giving out the relevant brand signals that you want for it to represent.

However, this begs the question of why organic traffic generated through quality copywriting is so important after all? Here are a few reasons:

There are two ways of getting your business to appear in the top search results – paying for ad spaces or SEO.

The traffic coming through paid ads is known as paid traffic. While the links appear below, these ads are known as organic results, and these generate organic traffic, which is free. The only required investment is content creation. While it may seem faster and simpler to generate traffic through paid ads, people are unaware of the tremendous benefits of organic traffic. Let's look at them, shall we?

Gets You Highly Qualified Leads

Businesses that appear on the first search results page receive around 92% of traffic, with the first result getting 33% of it. If your content is strategically SEO-optimized and ranks on the first results page, you boost the chances of getting qualified leads.

Organic Traffic has More Sustainability

A downside of paid traffic is that it comes only when you are paying to play. Anytime you stop spending money on ads, your traffic will stop. On the other hand, Organic traffic keeps on coming. While it does take some time to index your content and rank well but when that happens, you get significant benefits for a long time.

Gives You a Competitive Edge

Research proves that at least 87% of searches for products begin online, which means that if a business is dominating the search results, it will automatically take over the market. Also, if you aim to generate organic traffic, you do not have to spend more than your competitors in the marketing department. You just have to give your customers unique content, making it difficult for the competitors to win them over.

Users Trust Lies More in Organic Results instead of Sponsored Ones

Most people on the internet do not click on results that are sponsored. They know that paid ads are just there to "entice" them into clicking on the link of a brand.

Organic Results Build Your Brand

If you make good use of the SEO copywriting strategy, you will have plenty of web pages that rank well in the search results. This will enhance the brand awareness of your business among users and garner the trust of your audience once they see you as an authority in a niche. (Nkhoma, 2020)

1.3 Optimizing Your Content with SEO Copywriting

Here are 9 guidelines you can abide by to optimize your content with SEO copywriting.

1) Understanding and matching keyword intent

"Keyword intent" means the reason why people look for keywords that you are targeting. In general, three types of intents exist:

1. Informational: This is where users wish to learn about a topic, industry, or product, for example: "The history of Labor Day."

2. Navigational: Here, users want to visit certain websites and web pages. For example: "1800 flowers"

3. Commercial: This is where users want to purchase a service or product. For example: "Buy bouquets of flowers."

Since it is in a search engine's best interests to provide top-notch results to its users, engines like Google only reward marketers who match the keyword intent closely. Suppose a business is targeting the keywords "history of Labor Day" and using the pricing page for their flower delivery service. In that case, they will not perform well in terms of organic search results because they failed to match keyword intent.

Therefore, think about what your users require and then try your best to provide it to them.

2) Get to the point

The ultimate goal of SEO copywriting is to create content that is relevant and goes in the top organic results. To do this, mention your primary keywords early in the SEO copy. Means 50 words later in your SEO copy, your main keyword should already have been targeted three times.

3) Refrain from keyword stuffing

While keyword density is essential, do not overdo it. This is how it looks.

"Subject lines in Emails are important because subject lines in emails decide whether people read your emails. It is imperative to perform an A/B test on the subject lines in your emails." This SEO copy will be disregarded by both search engines and readers because nobody wants to engage with content created to just appease the algorithm.

4) Speak your audience's language

Take help from Keyword research tools such as WordStream to see keywords that are most searched during a period of time. This will help you know what your audience wants.

5) Shoot for the featured snippet

Research has proven that more than half of the Google searches end up without a click; these users leave the results without clicking on even one hyperlink. This highlights the importance of the featured snippet, which is a little box appearing at the top of your search results. It gives you some information about the product, which may be less but highly relevant information.

6) Think hard about your headline

If you do not have an engaging headline, users are less likely to go further on your website. Therefore, if you wish to see your organic traffic skyrocket and page views increase, spend some time brainstorming clicks headlines.

7) Optimize your Meta tags

While you should be creative in choosing headlines, remember that Google is likely to cut off a headline with more than 60 characters. Therefore, remember to be concise. To prevent the audience from seeing half-written headings and losing interest, you should also be thoughtful in your description, which is the text right below a URL.

8) Target ancillary keywords

This means that targeting a number of related keywords using a single piece of content permits you to bring in a more extensive yet relevant audience. With the aid of the Free Keyword tool in WordStream's and Google's suggested queries, you would be able to find all ancillary keywords needed to optimize your SEO copy.

9) Don't forget to optimize Voice search

While it is not as important to optimize the voice search feature, you also should not completely ignore this feature. It is estimated that about two-thirds of users between the ages of 25 and 49 use this feature in their voice-enabled phones and other devices at least once each day. (Patel, 2021)

Chapter 2: What Copy Pros Do Not Want You to Know

This chapter will discuss myths about copywriting, how to correct them, and a few major insights into copywriting.

2.1 Myths About Copywriting and How to Correct Them

1) Copywriting is writing

Some people believe that just because they can write a magazine article or a blog post, they are qualified enough to write a copy.

However, copywriting is quite different; it involves unique techniques, different resources, and a whole other environment. For example, when someone is writing a blog post, they will often link out internally and externally to relevant resources to improve SEO and maintain quality content. However, if you link out in copywriting, you will distract the users from what you need them to do: buy your product. Moreover, people believe that copywriting involves just the typing out of words onto a document. In contrast, the most important part of writing a copy is researching and analyzing your brand and customers.

So, for a copy to be compelling, the writer must first get a clear picture of what the brand stands for and hear the brand voice loud and clear. They should spend time understanding their target audience – their fears, pains, and aspirations, identifying the objectives of the campaign and how they can be delivered.

Then they may create an outline and finally write the copy. However, this too requires several rough drafts before the writer produces a version that is suitable to the customer's needs.

Copywriting is selling

While copywriting does involve selling, the truth is that not all pieces of copy you write would be a success. This is because copywriters are not minded readers. While they can showcase and communicate value to the potential customers of a business, copywriters need to rely on the owners of the company to get all relevant information. This information is required to put their sales message across in a manner that is the most authentic but concise. It includes product features, benefits, case studies, research on the target market, and everything else needed to design an offer that is compelling and value-driven. Therefore, copywriting is not just selling.

2) Copy is the most crucial factor

While the copy is an important element, what you also need is a viable product, a hungry market, and a compelling marketing strategy. Only then does a clear copy produce the desired results; otherwise, the big wins of a business and its losses are not attributed to just the copy alone.

3) The focus of a good copy is on the words

Contrary to popular belief, artificially enhancing the keyword density in your copy is not the way to excel at copywriting. While previously SEO experts recommended a 3%-5% density of keywords to gain an organic rank in a competitive search query, in today's age, anything above 1% would look pretty suspicious, and close to 2% would be a horrible read.

The truth is that Google is smart and immediately detects foul play if a writer has deliberately tweaked the keyword density of their copy. From the user's end, they will find your website to be robotic, and organic traffic for your website will be severely lost. Moreover, writers also assume that using big words makes them sound smart and professional. However, the exact opposite of this is true.

Copywriters should write in simple layman terms because their writing levels will depend on the education of the target audience. Generally, they would have to register for someone who has an 8th-grade reading level. Only then would all users be able to comprehend everything fully in their copy.

While the copy should not be too childish, it should also not be too pompous as that will put people off equally. A tool that can help you in this regard is Read-Able, which lets you see what reading level your content is at.

4) A consumer cares about you and your busines

They do not. They only care about what the business has to offer them, and that is why they hand you over their money. They do not care if you have been a part of the local Commerce Chamber for 20 years or how adorable your children are, therefore leave these things out of your copy. Copywriting is to make consumers believe that your product or service will fulfill their needs, even if those are perceived needs that you have created. Simply put, a copy should focus on the advantages of a product or service to consumers. So, while it is great that your business has been operating from the same place for the last 10 years, your consumers care only about how the business can make their lives better. (Mesmer)

2.2 Essential Insights into Copywriting

1) Do more research

As it happens, the greatest copywriters are usually the most avid researchers. When copywriters **research the audience's needs** and characteristics, they end up offering much greater benefits to the users. Content that is tailored to the likes of the users turns them into customers. While increased readership does not always indicate an increase in sales, it is a crucial step in the right direction as it helps build the credibility and authority of your online business.

2) Add greater interest

Experts say that when you are clueless about what to write next in your copy or how your draft can be made better, it is advised that you add interest. Meaning you tell the truth but in a fascinating manner. To do so:

- Make your copy visually appealing
- Include your distinct personality and unique selling propositions
- Tell stories
- Include controversy
- Use humor to make it less boring

3) Inject personality

Every brand has its unique style, voice, and USP or Unique Selling Proposition. Experts say that creating a personality that is "*sharply defined*" is a great way to differentiate your brand from that of the competitors and attain a greater market share. Before publishing your copy, ensure that it clearly depicts your brand's persona and values and matches your target audience's needs.

4) Speak the language of your ideal customer

Copywriting Pros say that if you are trying to convince people to buy your product or service, you should always use the language that this audience uses every day. Meaning the language through which they think and understand. This helps prospective customers get to know your brand, grow a fondness for it, and trust in it because they recognize themselves in your words. In the long run, this helps you connect with your audience and build long-lasting relationships with them

Focus on benefits

Copywriting Pros' advice is that writers should emphasize the benefits of the products instead of their features. Here is what some experts have to say:

- John Caples: "The greatest headlines are the ones that appeal to a reader's benefits."

- Eugene Schwartz L "Explain what the product 'does' and not what it is."

- Bob Bly: "All successful copies discuss benefits."

This copywriting tip is a simple solution when your copy is not going so well; just remember that every mentioned feature should lead to some benefit.

5) Ask questions to which readers can say "yes"

This age-old persuasion technique states that the more times your prospects say "yes," the greater their chances of saying "yes" are there. Copywriter such as Parris Lampropoulos uses this technique, whereby while writing their sales copy, they throw in a question from time to time. Still, often they phrase the question like a statement, one that gets prospective customers to nod their heads.

This is an indication that you have hooked them.

6) Appeal to emotion

The trick behind including emotions in a copy is for the writer to ask themselves: what may be the deepest desires of my prospective readers right now? While there are a number of emotions one can appeal to, the primary driving emotions, i.e., the deepest and strongest of them, are:

- Guilt

- Fear

- Anger

- Exclusivity

- Flattery

- Salvation

7) Use active voice

While reading a copy, users understand the use of active voice more easily, as it conveys the brand's message faster and better. On the other hand, passive voice makes the brand identity seem weak and commands less trust. For example, a passive sentence "More than 5000 customers have been aided by our services" would be much more effective in an active voice: "We have aided more than 5000 customers".

8) Include a solid call to action

The chances are that if you do not specifically ask your readers to do a specific task, they will not do it. Therefore, incorporate CTA's and, to make the most out of them, ensure that they:

- Match the persona of the buyer and what stage they are at in the buying cycle

- Offer something that holds value

- Offer prospective customers something they may actually need but are unaware of its need.

- Reiterate your emotional driver of choice as well as your most important benefit.

9) Evaluate your copy's ratio of "you" vs. "we"

Compelling copywriting always begins with your customers. People do not want to read websites that talk only about the business and the company; rather, copies that talk directly to the prospects achieve more results. Therefore, ensure that your copy is using "you" twice more than "we" or the brand name. This way, you will naturally divert attention towards your customer's desires and needs. Your copy would be stronger, and you will get greater traffic, leads, as well as sales.

Derek Halpern, an expert, says that it is essential to create headlines and introductions that are benefit-driven and include triggers. These involve a lot of "you" and talking directly to the audience so that they understand exactly what to expect from the business.

10) Don't be clever

Lastly, copywriters often like to do wordplay. While sometimes that is okay if it goes with your brand personality and the type of content, most of the time, being concise and clear brings greater results than being clever.

As copywriter Gary Bencivenga says:

"Effective copywriting is salesmanship, not clever wordsmithing. The more self-effacing and invisible your selling skill, the more effective you are. Copywriters who show off their skills are as ineffective as fishermen who reveal the hook." (5 Copywriting Tips & Tricks from the Pros, 2017)

Chapter 3: "HOBO" A Super Simple Secret Formula!

This chapter will elaborate upon the secret but simple copywriting formula: H.O.B.O.! It will also explain effective sale approaches that you can incorporate into your sales process.

3.1 A Beginner's Guide to Copywriting and SEO

Having briefly discussed SEO in the last chapters and having read some tips and tricks to improve your copywriting, you must know that not all copywriters understand SEO, even if it has been put on their résumé. So, if you are a company looking to hire a copywriter, you must ensure that they have both the strategic and technical knowledge to draft compelling copies and score high ranks in search engine results.

To understand SEO in more detail, we will start by reminding you of Maslow's hierarchy of needs. A theory in psychology that ranks human necessities beginning from the most fundamental ones such as water, air, and physical safety to more enhanced needs such as social belonging and esteem. In essence, you cannot achieve the top needs unless your fundamental needs are satisfied.

The same principle has been used to construct a pyramid that explains how you should move in the world of SEO. At the foundation, you need to ensure crawl accessibility so that engines can index or reach your content. The process of Crawling is the one through which search engines release a robot team called spiders or crawlers to discover new content. This content can include web pages, images, or videos, but all of this content is found through links.

Googlebots start by fetching some web pages, after which they follow the links present on these webpages and find newer URLs. Googlebots are GOOGLE'S web crawlers. A Crawler" is any program that is used to automatically scan and discover websites by following links from one webpage to another. Here the robots find new content and add it to the index. An index is a place where search engines store information good enough to be presented to searchers.

However, suppose you run a business and have found that some of the most important pages from your website are absent in the index or certain unimportant ones have been indexed. In that case, you can implement some optimizations to direct the Googlebot on how your webpage content should be crawled. This optimization requires you to ask the following questions,

Is your content hiding behind several login forms?

If your website needs users to sign in, fill forms, or answer some surveys before reaching certain content, the search engines would not see these protected pages.

Is text hidden within non-text content?

As a business, you should not use non-text media such as images, GIFs, and videos to display content that you want to see indexed. While some search engines recognize images, there is no guarantee that they will understand them at this stage.

To solve this problem of indexing and crawling, you can use the optimizations involving Robots Meta directives. These Meta tags are the directions you can provide to Google about how your web page should be treated. You can inform the crawlers of things such as " avoid indexing the following page in your search results." This instruction can be executed through the Robots Meta Tags in the <head> of HTML pages.

Now coming to another important aspect of SEO basics, which is Links. These help search engines figure out which URLs happened to be more trustworthy to be ranked higher in the search results. To do this, the number of links pointing towards a site was counted, which included both backlinks and internal links. Backlinks work similarly to real-life WoM (Word-of-Mouth) referrals, where if well-known people such as celebrities like your product and speak well of it to others. It encourages other people to also use your product. Here being online, the more natural backlinks your webpage has from high-trusted websites, the greater its chances are of ranking higher in the search results.

Now that you know how your business page can show up in the search results, it is time to determine the keywords targeted in your content. To do this, you will probably have some words in mind that you want to rank for, such as the names of your products and services, as well as any other subjects that your webpage addresses. These are essential seed keywords in terms of your research, so start there! Enter these keywords in a keyword search tool to find their average search volume per month and similar keywords.

Using a florist's example specializing in weddings, you would type "florist" and "wedding" into the research tool. You will discover other highly relevant and most searched for words such as:

- Wedding bouquets

- Wedding flower shop

- Bridal flowers

While you do want to choose words that the audience is most searching for, sometimes it might be more beneficial to target words with lower search volume as they are much less competitive.

Lastly, here are some tools you can use to determine the worth of a keyword and how much value it would bring to your website.

- Moz Keyword Explorer - Enter a keyword in the Keyword Explorer and receive information such as monthly search volume and other SERP features, for example, local packs and featured snippets that rank for that term.

- Google Keyword Planner - This Keyword Planner happens to be the most frequently used starting point for research on SEO keywords. However, it does limit the data on search volume by dumping keywords together in large buckets of the search volume range.

- Google Trends - This trend tool works great if you want to find seasonal fluctuations in a keyword. For example, the words "holiday packages" would peak in the summer break months. (The Beginner's Guide to SEO, 2021)

3.2 What is H.O.B.O, the Super Simple Secret Copywriting Formula?

A "Hobo" is defined as a street person or a vagrant. We chose this word because of its correspondence to a simpleton way of life, mainly because several online copywriting experts emphasize that a copy needs to contain ample fancy words and be complicated. While full-blown sales copies for expensive products can have abundant fancy jargon, an everyday sales copy used by the average marketer could be much easier and still receive high sales and conversions.

These experts do not tell you that only two elements carry out the main task in a sales letter; the Headline and the Bullet. Everything else in the letter can primarily serve as filler. Therefore, to bring this point home, HOBO stands for:

H = HEADLINE (Your attention grabber)

O = OPENING (Your golden promise)

B = BULLETS (Your bold list of benefits)

O = OFFER (Your close call to action)

While adding the Bullets and Headline helps your letter make sense, if you do not give a close call to action at the end, your reader would be confused about what he should do with all the hype created about your product throughout the letter

Moreover, there is a clear gap between the Bullets and Headlines which requires a bridge. The bridge would function as a "welcome mat" because it is at the "front door." Imagine a sign on the lawn that says "For Sale." This is your headline. Now you knock on the main door. Once inside, you are greeted with the benefits of this house. This is the task performed by Bullets step for the reader. As the prospective buyer roams around the house, he imagines ownership of that house right there. This is why we pile benefits over benefits in only one bullet; we want it to hit hard! Therefore, an opening is included to smoothen the transition between grabbing your reader's attention with a Headline and hitting him with the Bullets. It also connects them with promises of things in the future. However, in the end, we must ask for a sale and close the deal. Therefore, the last element, which is an Offer or a close, is also an important ingredient.

However, good copywriting alone is not enough. There is a marketing triangle. What you need is a hungry market that is passionate about a need and offers that fulfill that need. Below we will tell you how you can cater to that hungry market through sales while generating substantial returns

The Four Universal Strokes to incur Good Sales Fortune

The four steps of HOBO represent a cycle of energy that engages universal laws and ensures that being in sync with this dynamic brings substantial returns for sales copies. When the copywriter "understands" how one step is followed by another in a sequence, their logic becomes an intuitive insight; suddenly, they just understand the "rhythm" and "know" what is happening.

Take the example of an engine; the "intake" or the first stroke comprises a combination of air and fuel being forced into a cylinder. Once done, the valve is closed. This function can be attributed to the Headline, a volatile mix of self-interest and curiosity. Next, we have the "compression stroke" used to compress the air and fuel mix. It tries to amplify the contents it took in. This is your Opening which comprises a lead sentence, a promise, and a build-up of energy to prepare for the next action.

Thirdly, the "power stroke" comes, which occurs when the compressed volatile mixtures are ignited using a spark plug. This stroke is the primary power source of an engine and works the same as the Bullets ignite the benefits and light a fire inside the reader to explore these benefits. Lastly, an "exhaust stroke" removes residual matter from the power stroke, which completes the cycle. In HOBO, this is the close offer phase, the previous step activated the buying impulse, and here the reader is simply moving into action. However, without the previous efforts, the offer itself would not have been sufficient to derive measure. While the Offer provided a pathway for action, the Open formed a bridge between Bullets and Headline, and then the Offer produced a bridge between the purchase and the Bullets. However, since sales copywriting is the assembling of benefits. How does one identify the best benefits of their service or product?

The 21 minutes Benefit Explosions System

This will help you understand using the 12 benefit-producing strategies listed below.

Benefit Explosion #1: Brain Dump

Put a three-minute timer and write down all the benefits which come to mind fast.

Benefit Explosion #2: Benefit Stimulus Words

Set a timer of three minutes.

Look over your list of benefits and try thinking of more. For example, cheaper...faster...bigger... better... of the highest quality... and so on.

Benefit Explosion #3: Learn from the benefits of your competitors

Set a timer for three minutes. Brainstorm your three most significant competitors, what they do and what benefits they offer. Use your memory to write the answers.

Benefit Explosion #4: Learn from the Most Enthusiastic Customers

Set a timer for three minutes. Imagine three of your most satisfied customers and imagine what they would say if you showed them your product. You can also call your happy customers and write down whatever they say. This is a game-changing trick used by pro copywriters because, thanks to their enthusiastic customers, the copy basically writes itself.

Benefit Explosion #5: Check Out the Websites of Your Competitors

Set a time of three minutes

Visit your competitors' websites and observe their sales copies. If they seem interesting, save them to your desktop.

Benefit Explosion #6: Pull out "Hooks" from the Bullets of Competitors

Set a time of three minutes. Pick your favorite sales copy from the saved collection. Read each of the bullets, and extract one benefit from them which truly catches your attention. Do not copy their points word to word but take an idea. For example, if a benefit says the user can get an astonishing amount of work done really fast, see if this applies to your service or product, note it down.

Benefit Explosion #7: At Last, the Greatest of the Best Benefits

Set a timer of three minutes.

Now reread your lists and extract out the top most benefits. This final list you make will be called the "killer benefits" list, and these benefits would lie at the core of your marketing.

Some optional benefit-generating strategies are:

- Ask your friends what they think your product's top benefits might be, look up magazines and books on

Amazon.com to extract benefits from the book back covers and blurbs.

- Wear your customers' shoes for a day to see how they would react to the product.

Next, we have the

The Art of Headline "Swiping"

You have the option of 11 Headline Templates, but you can always "swipe" more of these from winning copies and adjust them according to your product.

An unwritten rule says that copywriters borrow from the headlines of others as long as they do not use these headlines in the same market. For example, the headline for a health service could be used in a golf market. However, before getting to the templates themselves, understand the universal formula for creating a great headline,

The "Uncle B.E.N."

(Benefit + Emotion + Novelty)

Step one: Offer a large benefit.

Step two: Press hard on negative emotions such as anger, frustration, fear, greed, need for approval.

Step three: Insert "novelty". This is a contradiction arising from mixing two elements that usually do not go together. It is unexpected and therefore catches the reader's attention.

Now, here are a few headline templates.

1) The "Startling News":

Hook: Give some news and a benefit.

Start by announcing... "At Last!... add in a new concept. Discovery in" Then add the shocking new fact..." Shocking news..."

2) The "Guaranteed How to"

Hook: Easiest to create.

Make a promise that the reader will face no risk or imply a hidden "How to" like in "Losing 20 Pounds in One Month."

3) The "Overwhelming Frustration"

Hook: All of us are frustrated at some point in our day, especially those suffering from a chronic problem that cannot be solved.

Therefore, this hook immediately grabs the reader's attention because of its relatability.

Before we move forward, let's clear a misunderstanding that many copywriters face between a benefit and a feature. You know bullets are important, but their power relies upon benefits instead of simply naming the product's features. The feature is what a product does, while the benefit is what it does for a customer. For instance, if you are selling an electric saw, your customer's life would be changed because they would now neatly cut plenty of wood. Therefore, the saw's features have little connection with its benefits.

Lastly, we will give you some tips to improve your bullet points.

The Targeted Magic Bullet Templates

Since every bullet caters to a different interest or segment of the market, so different readers may buy your product because of the appeal from different bullets. There is a simple recipe for creating a successful mini-headline for the bullet. It involves the "super benefit," the "curiosity generator," and the "unexpected twist." Perhaps the simplest way to generate curiosity is to omit some important information. For example, if the first bullet says "The blankety-blank..." the one right below it should say "The wiggly-Piggly..." and so on. On the other hand, if you simply put "Attention!..." heading in the next bullet, this will distort any visual rhythm present and pull out the reader from their subjective trance. They are likely to see your copy as "just a couple of small advertisements." Lastly, it is recommended that you alternate bold text with plain text. Therefore, if you write the first bullet in bold, the second should be plain; the third bold, and then follow the same sequence. (Mesmer, "The Forbidden Knowledge Archive")

3.3 Effective Sales Approaches You Can Incorporate into Your Sales Process

1) Premium sales approach

Everyone appreciates free gifts. Your potential customers would be no different. With this approach, you can offer them a promotional item or a giveaway in order to get them excited about your brand or product. This approach offers the primary advantage of attracting customers who were otherwise hesitant.

The said free gift could simply be a gift card or an item bearing some relation to your product and service. For example, if your product is a car, you could offer a year worth of free gas re-fills as a premium.

However, remember that this approach should only be used to make contact, do not use it as a part of every sales offer.

2) Product sales approach

If you are selling a product that is unproven or new for your prospect, it is better to provide them with a free sample or trial to help them evaluate your offer. This is an excellent way of showing value and establishing credibility.

3) Network sales approach

Whether your online business is B2C or B2B, developing relationships with prospective clients is crucial to this process. It allows you to strategically rely upon a list of your own professional and personal connections. No matter what your network's size is, these connections can provide you with qualified leads and solid referrals. You can start by identifying the most well-connected people in your surroundings who can guide you to many qualified leads. However, remember to use smart judgment and do not go through an entire list of contacts only to bother individuals who cannot provide solid leads.

4) Prescriptive sales approach

It is always helpful to give your customers all the information they might need to reach the correct decision. Results show that customer-centered salespeople procure more sales. However, the latest research says that giving customers additional information or multiple options often suppresses sales. To help this issue, the prescriptive approach requires that a sales professional gives a clear suggestion to customers for taking action, backing it — with a specific rationale. He explains any complex elements of the purchase to the customer upfront, and the purchasing department is also included for additional approval. This helps the customers see the representative as someone who is proactive and works to eliminate obstacles. (4 effective sales approaches to incorporate into your sales process, 2021)

Chapter 4: The Simple Secret That Turns Good Sales Copy into Great Copy

This chapter discusses how you can write a great sales copy and use it to procure valuable clients.

4.1 Why Is It Important to Know Your Market?

Having learned quite a few copyrighting techniques, it is important to recall that regardless of what technique you are using, profitable copywriting only happens when you demonstrate an empathetic and thorough understanding of the customer's needs and desires. If you are a conscious company looking into your customer's desires, this is the best marketing choice you can make.

Therefore, copywriting starts with researching the market and knowing what your customers or those of your client will respond to. This is called understanding the customer's pain points, finding out what sort of messages will grab their attention, and engaging them. It is also important that they stay interested until they are on the path towards making a purchase. For example, owners of online businesses often complain that their website is not generating sufficient leads. Once the websites are audited, common mistakes that are observed include neglect of user experience by their website design and the inability of their copy to address customers' pain points and evoke engagement. Simply put, their websites were wholly feature-driven and failed to acknowledge the customer's concerns. As mentioned earlier, no matter how great a product is or its number of features, entirely feature-driven copies are a big no.

Moreover, knowing your market or customer intimately helps you understand what prices they are willing to pay, are comfortable shopping around, or prefer more impulse purchases. This is true when a conflict arises, an action which causes problems that need to be fixed by a reaction: their car breaks down, they need to go somewhere — they ring up a mechanic. Here you find out how desperate your customers are to solve their problems. Do they want to translate it as soon as possible, or are they okay with the solution taking time? Also, in a market, there may be other businesses offering services of the same nature. So, do these people trust you as compared to your competitor, and why? This research will guide you towards new approaches that you can use to present offers to prospects. If you find out that your customers like to shop around and prefer reading plenty of information prior to making a purchase decision, you can create a copy that caters to this need.

4.2 Responsibilities of Marketers and Copywriters

It can be easy to think that copywriters simply spend their time writing innumerable copies. However, the typical responsibilities included in a copywriters' job description can vary greatly. The tasks they perform range from research to writing to optimization and collaboration. Standard duties incorporate the following:

1) **Researching Concepts**

For many copywriters, every project they do starts with them being handed over a creative brief followed by an extensive session of research. First, they read through this creative brief and try to get a gist of what their client or boss wants them to accomplish.

Then the research begins. As per the nature of the project, they might review the analytics of their website to understand the behavior of users or interview long-term customers to see how they make their buying decisions. Another option is also to review testimonials and gauge the likes and dislikes of their target market.

Then the copywriters analyze their research to come up with some conclusions, such as the type of message that should be conveyed and what kind of tone should be used.

2) Writing Copy

This one may be obvious, but apart from research, a major responsibility of copywriters is writing both for print and digital use. Some common types of copies that they might produce include:

- Webpages, such as sales pages, homepages, articles, or blogs

- Brand taglines or product descriptions.

- Video or printed sales letters.

- Social media captions and email marketing.

Besides incorporating keywords for search engine optimization, copywriters may also have to meet other guidelines, such as strict requirements for word counts or length.

3) Collaborating with Colleagues

Something you might not know; copywriters hardly work alone. They usually work in close contact with the public relations, marketing, advertising, sales, and editing departments. Some of them also work with clients who may own businesses or company executives.

Therefore, copywriters often meet these people to share ideas and produce creative briefs. If their projects include other media types, like videos and illustrations, they may want to collaborate with photographers or designers to complete their tasks successfully.

4) Analyzing and Optimizing

When they undertake projects, copywriters usually strive to meet ambitious goals. For blog articles and webpages, key performance indicators may include a specific number of viewers or fresh subscribers over some length of time. For sales letters or pages, KPIs focus on the number of orders, sales numbers, customer retention, and new customers. KPIs are Key Performance Indicators. They are the metrics that marketers use to evaluate the factors that ensure the success of their business, for example, the number of new and returning visitors, top 5 search queries, and bounce rate.

Copywriters may closely track these results from their campaigns and then make adjustments for improving outcomes. Some copywriters use split tests to test with various versions of a copy and see which of those performs best. Once they have sufficient data to decide a winner, copywriters can complete their campaign through the running of the optimized version.

However, apart from marketing their products, copywriters' tasks can also include the following:

- Interview

- Proofread

- Edit

- Source images

- Manage Projects

- Gauge the broader impact of their work

- Plan as well as implement marketing campaigns

However, there can also be much more to the role of a marketing copywriter, for example, SEO strategizing, making videos, and social media planning. While a copywriter creates content, a marketer's job is to take that content and use it as a tool for generating site traffic and then leads. The latter refers to potential customers providing information about them to the business to stay connected, like an email address.

The crux is that even though words are the primary output for copywriters, writing is not what they spend most of their time doing. They have to incorporate plenty of research, tweaking, thinking, and formatting. (Dodd, 2021)

4.3 The Key to Writing a Killer Sales Copy

While you know how to write a sales copy, these copies often seem too dry to tour readers and may put them to sleep. Not saying that you should make your sales page into a thriller novel, but it is okay to play with words and give the users a reason to continue reading. Your sales copy should present whatever you are selling in such an attractive way that the readers cannot say "no." Here is how you can do that:

1) Choose one focus

Your target audience would have a certain goal, a pain point, or a desire. They may have secondary goals or pain points, but you just need to pay attention to one and make your pitch. For example, a prospective customer who is complaining of the failure of his air conditioning system may have a pain point from those listed below:

- Uneven cooling

- High electricity bills

- No link between the thermostat and the air conditioner.

- Frustration due to non-environmentally-friendly Air conditioners

You can mention all of these in your copy, but it is better to stay focused on only one depending on the customers' persona and your own data collection on customers. This way, you would avoid overwhelming your readers with excessive information.

2) Define your goal

You wish to sell a product, but is there a specific sales goal that you have in mind for your page? For example, do you intend to sell a single product, a bundle of products, or a pricier version of those products? Choose the desired action and then push your customers towards it through your sales copy.

Also, highlight your goals with regard to conversions. Before writing a sales copy, put it to the test in front of several consumers; that should give you a fair idea of your baseline conversion rate. You can also use historical sales figures or informed guesses to determine the percentage of visitors converted to sales on your page.

3) Use compelling words

Avoid boring language that will drive your readers away, instead come up with ways you can captivate your audience and sustain their attention.

Consider these sales copies written to convince consumers to purchase a new air conditioner:

- Are you ready to replace your old Air conditioner? We offer a wide variety of products that fit your needs, as well as free in-home consultations where you can meet licensed technicians. Select a new Air conditioner today and begin reaping the advantages of cool air.

- It is late in the afternoon, the hottest day of this summer, and suddenly air stops coming through your vents. All the word's fans in would not prevent you from sweating inside your own house, so you scramble to get a technician to replace or fix your air conditioner. Don't allow this to happen to you!

The second copy draws a picture and hits the customer's pain point. As a result, they will immediately recall the panic that erupted when they had an AC disaster.

4) Make it readable

Readability can be about several factors:

- Relatable language

- Bold copy to indicate essential points

- Plenty of negative space

- Storytelling

5) Creating an attractive CTA (call to action)

Every sales copy requires an easy-to-see yet attractive call to action. Try using a button to make it more eye-catching. Call to action for a business explaining the advantages of an Air conditioner might be one of these:

- Discover more comfort at a lesser cost

- Spend less on energy bills from today

- Schedule free consultations

Having read the above tips for great copywriting, you are halfway through the journey. However, you still need to know a few more secrets.

The secret to high-impact sales copy

While you do need to write powerful sales copies that follow certain sales structures, you also have to engage the readers' imagination throughout your copy. This means that if users are on your sale pages, they perhaps already desire what you are selling or are considering its purchase.

Your task is only to help these people see them benefiting from using your product. That is how you will win their sale. Also, because individuals usually buy due to emotional reasons, rather than practical ones, you can use the following secret techniques in your copy:

a) Imagining happiness

Suppose there is a headline for a sales copy that says, " Imagine a life where you cannot wait to wake up each morning'. The readers' imagination would start as soon as they read this, and then you to direct this imagination in the right direction by speaking of the desire to become a successful writer. For your audience, this dream would be so elusive; they would not imagine what it is really like, so tell them what it feels to be an in-demand writer, thereby giving blood and flesh to the offer of writing professionally. The crux is that many a time, a goal you mention in the sales copy may be vague even for those aspiring for the goals. So, add details to help users see their dream more clearly.

b) Imagining success

Speaking of dreams, before you begin writing, you should brainstorm the extent of the emotional baggage coming with the readers' dreams. You would want to know why they have these dreams. What are their feelings about their life right now? Then consider how your product will address these feelings. Essentially, at least one part of your copy should be dedicated to addressing these feelings.

Notice the emotional temperature of this copy. For example, if your business sells eyeglasses, you can write an emotionally loaded sales copy that addresses your customer's self-esteem, finances, and goal-setting. This gives the reader an impression that regardless of their problem or how they want to fix it, your product will take care of it.

c) **Imagine the life-long dream: Allow the readers to complete the picture**

To sum it up, the use of "Imagine" is a powerful technique. Still, instead of pushing his own idea of success onto his readers, a copywriter tickles their imagination and motivates them to paint their own picture. Most of your customers will already have an idea of what happiness or success looks like for them; your job is just to let them pull this picture out and think how your product can fit into that picture. However, avoid sounding manipulative. While your customers might pull out their dreams, they would not want you to tarnish them with over-the-top selling tactics. (Mesmer, The Forbidden Knowledge Archive)

Therefore, to prevent any such selling mishaps, here are some useful principles for copywriting:

7) Never-fail principles for copywriting

1) Know who you are talking to

Imagine your customers include a teenager, a backpacker, and a busy mother. You would have to talk differently with each of these people, meaning you cannot write the same sales copy for everybody.

Instead, design a persona for your customer, describe them and assign them a name. Imagine what they may be like, how they might spend their days, or what the issues in their life may be. Only then can you write an excellent sales copy.

2) Writing to a friend (wife, colleague, etc.)

Copywriters should not forget that they are dealing with real people. Even if the business is selling B2B products, there will always be a person involved who has an identity and a name and will be making decisions after reading your copy. Therefore, forget to use complicated jargon or buzzwords such as social media management systems which do not mean anything. Instead, employ the friend test, meaning read the copy, and if there is a sentence that you would not say in conversation with a friend, remove it or change it.

3) Working hard to create a compelling headline

Most people do not read; they just skim. However, all of them read the headline. Therefore, ensure that your headline captures their attention and interest.

These are the questions you should think of while writing a great headline:

- What do your prospects care about more than anything?

- What is their most pertinent problem?

- What is their biggest dream or goal?

- How can you guide them in achieving their goal or solving their problem?

4) **Don't make them think**.

Contrary to what is commonly believed, your readers do not want to think a lot. They want to view your copy and understand whatever you are offering. If your idea is not apparent at the start of the copy, your readers will quit and reading move on. So, while your primary headline is benefit-oriented, below the headline, describe in a few lines:

- What the product is.

- What the product does.

- Who the product is for.

5) **Avoiding all caps and exclamation marks**

Writing plenty of words using all caps or the bold feature will slow down the customer's reading, interest, and comprehension. In contrast, text in lower case happens to be recognized quicker than all caps. Also, using two or three exclamation marks together shows a lack of maturity and depth instead of drawing attention to your point, which takes away from it.

6) Readability matters

If you wish for customers to go through your text, ensure that it is readable. Key things that improve readability:

- **Font size**: Minimum 14px, preferably 16px;

- **Start a new paragraph after 3–4 lines:** Leave an empty line between each new paragraph

- **Line height**: 24px;

- **Using sub-headlines:** After every second or third paragraph

- **Line width**: Maximum 600px. People will not read your copy if the lines are too long.

- **Use images to break your text apart.** People will read more if you break the patterns from time to time.

- **Using darker text on a lighter background:** Black text with a white background is ideal.

7) Sales copies should only be as long as necessary

If users are not interested in your product or service, it would not matter how long your sales copy is. If your customers seem interested, provide them with all information they require, but they can skip some parts of the sales copy to click "Buy" instead of reading the whole thing. On the other hand, if you make them read the entire sales copy and they are still not convinced, then you would have a problem.

Lastly, in today's day and age, standing up for a cause is not just considered good citizenship but intelligent business. At least 66% percent of users are more inclined to spend on a product that a sustainable brand makes. Therefore, conscious companies today try to get their customers enthusiastic about whatever change they would help make by buying their product or service. This is done by designing a clear and compelling copy that speaks to the customer. However, businesses often get caught up in one of these two traps while communicating their corporate responsibility or social missions. (Laja, 2019)

a) The "Nonprofit Nap" Trap

When profit-earning companies try to include corporate responsibility in their mission, they often start using clichéd non-profit jargon. For example, a tech company might write in their copy "historically underserved populations" or "empowering minorities while bridging the tech diversity gap," but people would have little idea what this means or how it relates to tech business. While jargon can be helpful if the company is writing to get a grant approved, it alienates the people the company was supposed to inspire into signing up for their products and services.

b) The "Quiet Cause" Trap

Companies that treat their social responsibility like an afterthought leave their customers in the dark about whether their dollars will help fund a cause close to their hearts or not.

To overcome these traps and turn your yawn-worthy copies into engaging stories that boost business:

- **Put what you believe front and center**

Instead of pushing their beliefs to an isolated corner, your "About" page should bring them into the spotlight. For example, the website for Sweet green restaurant has a prominent section on food ethos where they write, "we believe the choices we make about what we eat, where it comes from, and how it is prepared to have a direct and powerful impact on the health of individuals, communities, and the environment." This is the "TED Talk" formula, which efficiently communicates the big idea your business wants to spread. (Weaver, 2018)

Chapter 5: The Instant Sales Letter Template

This chapter will inform you about how to set SEO performance in sales letters. You will also be given a brief introduction to the instant sales letter template!

5.1 Introduction to Instant Sales Letter Template

A sales letter includes these parts

1. **Introduction:** This is the beginning of your sales letter. You have to ensure that all facts concerning your businesses' history, expertise, experience, market demand, and products or services are mentioned here in a concise manner.

2. **Statement of Purpose:** This is a description of one line narrating the subject of your letter, which can be your product, new offers, or services.

3. **Description:** This is the middle and perhaps the trickiest part of a sales letter. Remember not to show over-confidence, over-excitement, or exaggeration in this section. Only focus on the letter's subject, narrate why customers should be investing in your business, and how your business promises quality. Try to be as engaging and

as specific as possible by adopting a conversational but persuasive style.

4. **Statement of benefits:** Talk about the advantages and perks that the subject of your letter provides to the customers.

5. **Pitch:** The entire sales letter ultimately leads to this part. Here you persuade your readers sufficiently for them to contact your business if they want more details on the subject of the letter.

   - Apart from these larger sections, sales letters also comprise modules or units which fit together like pieces of a puzzle and have a unified impact. These chunks are the

   - Headline

   - Opening

   - Bullets

   - Offer

As explained earlier in the book, once you comprehend all these elements and their value to the letter, it becomes easy to take them apart and put them back together. Like in an engine, you can take the parts apart and observe the defective or working features. Then you put it back together, hoping that it will work.

However, it often takes years and costs a large fortune just to determine the correct combinations to make the sales letter work; many of these letters fall flat regardless of the investment you have made. So instead of wearing themselves out trying to produce the correct sales copy, one can have an extensive collection of profit-generating and hard-hitting sales letters for their business, ready at their demand. You simply have to go to these websites and click on your required niche, for example, Business to Business. Instantly you will have access to lead-generating letters that pull in several interesting prospects. (How to Write a Persuasive Sales Letter to Drive More Sales (20+ Samples), 2020)

These are known as Instant Sales Letters

They are a collection of sales letter templates designed to provide you with 'fill-in-the-blanks ready-made letters for all kinds of businesses or other 'selling' purposes.

Available from several credible sources online, these templates could be from one of these eight categories:

- Information Products

- Retail/Restaurants

- Professional

- Service

- Business to Business

All that is required of you is to insert your company's details and those of the service/ product you provide to these 'gaps.' You do not have to worry about writing anything on your own. Copywriters know that a powerful letter is synonymous with having an automatic, money-making machine working tirelessly for you. However, creating a winning letter is the tricky part, which is helped by these sales letter templates.

Below is a sample template:

From,

_____

_____

Date (Date on which letter is written)

To,

_____

_____

Sub: _____

Dear _____, (name of the recipient)

We are glad to inform you that _____

_____ (introduce your company and products on sale and also mention the discounts prevailing).

Our company _____ (provide your company history and mention the offers).

So, what are you waiting for? Grab this special offer?

Thanking you,

Yours sincerely,

(_____)

Such templates usually take no more than 2 minutes to fill up and are super effective for maintaining record speed. An example of such a service being offered online is that Yanik's Instant Sales Letters kit. (Silver, 2020)

5.2 Formula for High-Converting Headline Copywriting

Since you know what value a great headline holds for a sales copy, let's learn how you can write winning Headlines using just 9 Steps:

1) Understand your target. Prior to writing a sales copy, especially if your goal is a substantial ROI, you need to understand your target audience. For example, the editors for Cosmopolitan understand clearly, their readers and therefore, their headlines target the reader's emotions ideally.

2) Start with writing an outline for your ad first. Then move to the headline.

3) Write several headlines and read all of them out loud.

4) Choose the most significant benefit provided by your product and include it in your headlines.

5) Incorporate the problem or the product in your headlines.

6) Use one of these formulas for headlines:

Are you _____?

"Are You Ready to Have the Gorgeous Lawn within Your Neighborhood?"

Only use these question headlines if their answer is evident to your reader.

"How I _____"

"How I Defeated Joint Pain, Came Off from the Sidelines and Right Back into the Game."

"How to _____"

"How You Can Add about 20 Yards in Your Drives and Hit the Ball in the Fairway More Often than a PGA Tour Pro."

7) Use a standard and straightforward headline using one of these or other formulas

8) It is okay to write a whacky, ultra-different, or off-beat headline, even though it may fail several times; occasionally, it might beat your 'normal' headlines from #7.

9) Keep testing your headlines constantly and rewrite them when you observe some decline in response.

Here are some examples of Persuasive headlines with high conversion rates:

1. Check now and get [number]% OFF

2. Win a $[number] gift card

3. Get [number]% off your first order

Here are some ideas for Urgency headlines:

These headlines inculcate a feeling of urgency and push the readers to take action.

1. Last chance! [number]% off all products ends tomorrow!

2. Watch out for our exclusive offers – here only for a limited time!

3. Free shipping for completing your purchase in 15 minutes

Now, let's move to another integral element of HOBO, the B, or bullet points. (Lorincz, 2021)

What are bullet points?

These are used for listing out items in your sales copy. They help to communicate a message effectively by capturing the reader's attention of readers. Especially those who do not want to read through lengthy copies but simply scan through.

Here's how you can write bullet points that people want to read:

a) In the bullet, express a prominent benefit and a promise to your reader

Bullets are, in fact, mini-headlines. They encourage the reader to scan through your copy, go to the actual content in your sales copy or take action using the call to action.

b) **Keep the bullet points symmetrical**

Your Bullet points should only be one line or two lines each. It is easier on the eyes and so easier for the reader.

c) **Avoid clutter of bullets**

Do not get lost in a complex jumble of bullets, subtitles, and sub-bullets. Bullets should provide clarity and not confusion.

d) Practice parallelism

Ensure that any bullet groups in your copy are thematically related. Start every bullet with the same element of speech and keep up a unified grammatical form.

e) Bullets do not have to be sentenced

If you wish to write whole sentences, choose a numbered list or a paragraph. (Bruce, 2021)

Chapter 6: Tips, Tricks, and Trends

This chapter will provide insight into changes that readers can use to create killer copywriting that'll transform any business.

6.1 Copywriting Tips to Keep the Readers Glued to Your Screen

Coming full circle, we understand that writing can be hard work, while some days your writing flows; on others, it is torturous to get anything out on the paper. However, here are some killer tips for copywriting that will boost your business like no other:

1) Proven methods net proven results

The idea that some of us are just born with exceptional copywriting genes is a myth. Even if you struggle with copywriting, there are numerous copywriting formulas to make your life easier, for instance. One of the most popular is the PAPA formula which stands for:

The problem, advantages (of solving the problem), proof (that you can solve it), and action

First, the copywriter presents a problem which is the pain point or need of their customers. For example, "the struggle of finding your dream job."

Then, the writer moves in with the reasons why the customers need their problem fixed. For example, "years of effort in vain" or trying to avoid the "resume black hole."

Next, provide proof of the problem being solved by your product; for example, "Hundreds of students used it and got results."

Then seal the deal with an action-oriented task, such as making the customers watch a video, click a CTA, sign up for your lead magnet.

2) Eliminate powerless words

These are the words that cause your content to look lifeless and your visitors to question why they begin reading this sales copy at all. They also dilute the essential meaning of your content and hijack excessive space without providing any actual value. Here is an example:

Advanced planning. Or *planning in advance.*

Both look harmless but do not be fooled. Both these words are redundant because planning is doing something prior to the event. So, there is no point in adding the word "advance" since its meaning is already signified by the word "planning."

3) Set a word count

Remember to be precise with words. Your consumers do not have the time to read through a whole book; in fact, as per research, you have just 7 seconds to make a great first impression online. Have clean thinking and use simple language to draft copies that resonate with your target audience and motivate them to purchase.

4) Notice your messaging hierarchy

Some writers are in the habit of burying the most significant thing they have to say. This mistake happens because:

The writer is unprepared and just blurted out the copy.

The owner of the business is oblivious to the downside of long and dry introductions. To ensure your message is heard, adopt this strategy:

1. Choose a web page from your website.

2. Brainstorm and write down everything that needs to be said.

3. Jumble the order of this list until you are satisfied with the message hierarchy.

4. Reframe your copy by using opposites

There is so much material on the web that it has become impossible to retain a viewer's attention in this day and age. To make it through all this noise, you can use opposites to pull people out of their comfort zones. Taking the example of dieting, everyone knows that eating more vegetables helps lose weight, but this is what every page says. To catch the reader's attention, you could reframe such information. For example, the main problem with eating healthy is avoiding all sugary foods, but this lasts only a week. So, people would be better off if they were permitted to eat sweets on alternative days. Therefore, you could say: *Want to lose weight by eating chocolate?*

Combining the subject of dieting with a fairly unrelated topic [chocolate], you immediately capture your reader's attention. (Patel, 6 Copywriting Tips That'll Keep Readers Eyes Glued to Your Screen, 2019)

6.2 How Can You Jumpstart Your Creativity

Staring at an empty page can be stressful when you are running short of time and need to write an excellent sales copy. To help your creativity flow, we have listed down these tested and tried trips:

1) Try a 10-minute free-write

If you are unable to write product descriptions or headlines, give your mind a break and try free writing for some time.

Freewriting requires timed and continuous writing without any oversight or feedback. This means that you need not worry about grammar or about getting off the topic. There is, in fact, no need to set a topic or show someone what you write.

2) Find some data

Copywriting requires plenty of research. Therefore, take your time reading industry sources about your topic, going through relevant threads on Twitter, and interviewing an expert to gain interesting data.

Even if this research does not help you write your copy, having this background would strengthen your copywriting skills, and you will soon write copies that sell.

3) Skip the introduction for a while

If you are struggling to start, it is ideal to jump right into the first topic while skipping the introduction altogether.

The purpose of an introduction is to establish a tone for the copy, introduce the topic, and mold expectations for the reader. It tells you what subjects the copy will touch, how these subjects would be arranged, and what the reader will learn after they are finished. So naturally, before writing the piece, you would not know any of this and cannot tell your reader what to expect. Therefore, skip the introduction and get back to it once your scope is clear and the remaining content is written.

4) Rewrite your favorite ad

A great way to begin writing is, to begin with, something else. If there is an ad campaign you love, grab its copy, watch the ad, read the copy, and then rewrite it. Try reworking this ad campaign to make it more relevant to your business. (Clark, 2021)

6.3 Quick & Actionable Tips to Improve SEO and Earn Higher Search Rankings

Plenty has changed in the universe of search engine optimization. However, some fundamental principles remain unchanged.

1) Remove Anything Slowing Down Your Site

The speed of your page is critical in SEO. Previously, one could do business with a slow-loading website, but in today's market, it is the kiss of death. Slow pages will frustrate customers and discourage them from purchasing your product. While businesses are becoming more enthusiastic about increasing revenue through SEO and optimizing to generate leads, the demand for speed is also massively increasing. A slow page means you are far behind in the list of websites developing organic traffic, regardless of your content quality or site design.

2) Write for Humans First, Search Engines Second

Lately, a number of copywriters have been reversing to outdated methods of SEO, where keywords were given more importance than whether the content was engaging and valuable. A number of people still do not capitalize on long-tail keywords. Instead, they prefer the manipulation of search engines. This is a fruitless approach. Write content for the humans reading your copy, individuals who have eyes for reading, and credit cards for purchasing your product. Remember that search spiders are merely scripts — they do not buy products, engage with your business on social media, and do not become loyal customers.

3) Encourage Other Trustworthy Sites to Link to You

No matter what has changed, inbound links still happen to be the lifeblood of rankings on search engines. Once you combine the nofollow and dofollow links, you obtain a natural link profile which is rewarded by Google. (Patel, Neil Patel)

Conclusion

Now that you have read the book, you know enough about SEO to boost the rankings of your online business or have a business rank high in the search results. You started by learning the inner workings of Search Engine Optimization and all that entails copywriting. In each chapter, the book imparted you with several lesser-known secrets to great copywriting, along with tips on writing great headlines, readable bullet points, and a copy that does not make your readers bored as several copies do. The most crucial takeaway perhaps was the acronym HOBO, which lies at the center of all great copywriting as it pertains to four essential parts of any copy: the headline, the opening, the bullets, and the offer. The book then has reiterated that regardless of how skilled of a writer you are, you must know your market and customers through and through to write an excellent copy. This has been accompanied by expert sales approaches, which in my vast experience, always work. You have also learned the formula for high conversion headlines, exercises to get your creativity flowing, instant templates for sales letters when you are short of time, and several actionable tips to improve SEO and earn higher search rankings.

All in all, you can say that you are now ready to hone your skills as a copywriter, and with the added knowledge of SEO, your business will soon be up in the stars.

Lastly, if you have enjoyed the book, please leave a review on Amazon.